D1364923

2014

Take care of the birds!

Happy Birthday, Lexa —

Love + God bless,

Omi

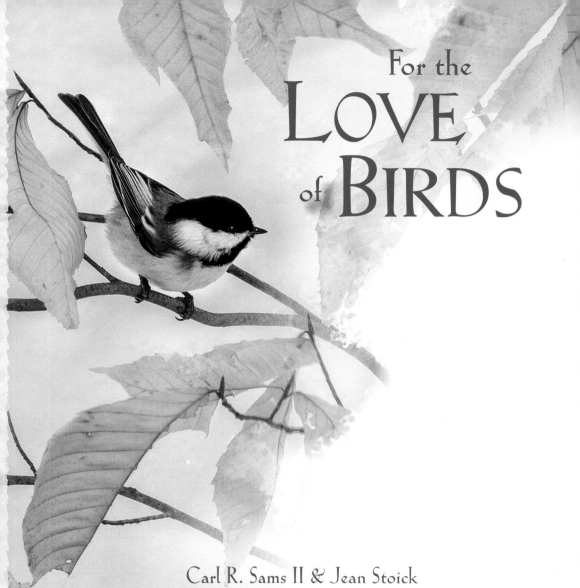

For the
LOVE
of BIRDS

Carl R. Sams II & Jean Stoick

Acknowledgements

We would like to thank our loyal staff: Karen McDiarmid, Becky Ferguson,
Bruce Montagne, Kirt Manecke, and Sandy Higgins for their contributions in the creation of this book;
Thanks to color specialist, Greg Dunn;
Thanks to our apprentice, Erick Whitford for the use of his female cardinal image.

Publisher
Carl R. Sams II Photography, Inc.
361 Whispering Pines
Milford, MI 48380
800/552-1867 248/685-2422   Fax 248/685-1643
www.strangerinthewoods.com   www.carlsams.com

Karen McDiarmid — Art Director

Sams, Carl R.
For the Love of Birds
by Carl R. Sams II & Jean Stoick, Milford, MI
Carl R. Sams II Photography, Inc. © 2013

Summary: A photographic collection
of North American birds.

Printed and bound June 2013 — #84842
Friesens of Altona, Manitoba, Canada

ISBN 978-0-9827625-4-7

Birds (North American)
Library of Congress Control Number: 2013908456

10 9 8 7 6 5 4 3 2 1

Dedicated to
those who protect
wild places and
care for our
feathered friends.

Male
Baltimore Oriole

Baltimore orioles are insect and fruit eaters.
Cut oranges in half in spring to attract these striking
orange and black birds to your own backyard.

Female Mallard Duck

Male Mallard Duck

The mallard duck is
North America's most
abundant duck.

Blue Jay

American Robin

Blue Jay

Hairy
Woodpecker

Red-headed
Woodpecker

Snow geese and one lone crane lift off during migration.
They stir up the wind with thousands
of thundering wingbeats.

Sharp-tailed
Grouse

During spring,
male sharp-tailed grouse
gather in early dawn light
to perform
energetic,
rhythmic
dances to
attract the
females.

Female
Ruby-throated Hummingbird

Snowy Owl

The female snowy owl
is peppered with dark markings;
the male is primarily white.

Canada Goose

Canada geese
mate for life.
The pair stays together
throughout
the year.

The common raven is considerably larger than the American crow.

Common
Raven

The crow is believed to be the most intelligent bird,
mastering complex vocalizations.
His sharp call will warn other wildlife
of approaching danger.

Male wild turkeys
in display.

Male
Indigo Bunting

Thistle seed is a magnet for attracting goldfinch.
With patience and luck, you may also see
an indigo bunting.

Male
American Goldfinch

Mute swans are fierce protectors
of their cygnets.

Mute Swans

Bohemian waxwings are slightly larger than cedar waxwings. The Bohemian has the rust coloring under his tail, a blush of rust on his face, as well as a red, white and yellow wing bar.

Cedar Waxwing

Bohemian Waxwings

Great Egrets

Territorial disputes can erupt over nesting rookeries
during the breeding season.

During the early 1900s, highly prized
egret feathers adorned ladies' hats.
The Audubon Society was formed to prevent egrets
and other birds from being hunted

into extinction.

Both hooded mergansers and wood ducks
are cavity-nesters.

Male & Female
Hooded Mergansers

Male Wood Duck

Male Scarlet Tanager

Male Cape May
Warbler

Sandhill
Crane

California Quail
(prey)

Red-shouldered Hawk
(predator)

Green Herons

The clever little green heron is known to
drop bait into the water to attract small fish.

Great Horned
Owl

The great horned owl is named for
its distinctive ear tufts.
They are one of the earliest nesters.

Add some peanuts to
your feeder to attract
this little nut lover.

White-breasted
Nuthatch

Mourning
Dove

Black-capped
Chickadee

Great Blue
Heron

Great blue herons are widely found
throughout North America.

During breeding season the male
red-winged blackbird is fiercely territorial.
He aggressively chases away other
males and sometimes challenges predators
much larger than himself.

Red-winged
Blackbird

Ring-necked
Pheasant

The ring-necked pheasant
is easily identified by its bold markings.
It was introduced as a game bird from Asia.

Rose-breasted
Grosbeak

Colorful grosbeaks have
large, strong beaks used for cracking seeds.

Evening
Grosbeak

American Bald Eagles

The female American bald eagle
is usually larger than the male.
This is common among raptors.

Male
Northern Cardinal

Female
Northern Cardinal

Mandarin ducks were
imported from China to adorn
the Hollywood ponds of an early era.
Now they populate
areas of the west coast.

Mandarin
Duck

Barred Owl